PRAISE for MARC

Critò di Volta is the astonishing prophecy of a turn in our direction, from present-day triviality and self-contempt to a new life of imaginative joy and the superb energy of peace, the one true energy. "We must wake soon or sleep unto our deaths," the poem cries. And elsewhere, it sings the cure, "It is harder for the unloved to love, so let us love the unloved the most ..." Marc di Saverio has somehow brought forth a culture-creating epic which at the same time is the imaginative biography of the suffering outcast of our time, of his family, his loved ones, and the world he loves, and also of what threatens these loves: our blind yet willful self-defeat. A prophecy, an epic, but also a novel in verse (and prose! and pictures!), a gallery of portraits, a fountain of images. A powerful unity of purpose within a harmonized kaleidoscope of new forms, both free and structured. A completely original mastery of the art of poetry. A work of genius. Perhaps di Saverio's poem is most of all a white-hot fusing of love and anger, tenderness and brutal honesty, realism and hope, analytical insight and soaring vision. Or perhaps above all, *Critò di Volta* is a treasure-house of beauty: "And her vermilion hair, / curved along her forehead like the blade of an ancient sword, / quavered." Or perhaps above all it is a quest and achievement of love on every page, as it embraces "black gleams of distance / and dolour I too share in loving her."

> —**A.F. Moritz** (Griffin Poetry Prize winner, Guggenheim Fellow, and Poet Laureate of Toronto)

Di Saverio's imagination belongs in the company of Blake, Pound, Rimbaud and Nelligan, among others.

> —**Darren Bifford** (poet and professor), *Arc Magazine*

Di Saverio's *Sanatorium Songs* is the greatest poetry debut from the past 25 years.
> —*Canadian Notes and Queries*

Crito di Volta is absolutely superlative. It is rather sweet irony that the first poetic masterpiece in the English language of the 21st century should be published almost exactly 100 years after the great modern epics *Ulysses* and *The Wasteland*.

   —**Peter O'Neill** (Irish poet and critic)

Armed with a cigarette in one hand and the words of the Almighty in the other, *Crito di Volta*, a troubled visionary, is leading a 21st-century revolution unparalleled since the times and teachings of Christ. Through his vivid and transformative poetic imagery, raw accountability, and dream of a future delivered from Evil, Marc di Saverio delivers an uncompromising manifesto for our blasted heath of a world—even if the angels have to go off their medications.

   —**Rod Carley** (author and actor)

Marc di Saverio is one more poet to hit Eliot's formidable mark.

   —**Laura Lush** (GG-nominated poet and critic), *Modern Literature Magazine*

SONGS OF MY SURRENDERS

ESSENTIAL POETS SERIES 307

 Canada Council Conseil des Arts
for the Arts du Canada

ONTARIO ARTS COUNCIL
CONSEIL DES ARTS DE L'ONTARIO

an Ontario government agency
un organisme du gouvernement de l'Ont

Guernica Editions Inc. acknowledges the support of the Canada Council
for the Arts and the Ontario Arts Council. The Ontario Arts Council
is an agency of the Government of Ontario.

We acknowledge the financial support of the Government of Canada.

MARC DI SAVERIO

SONGS OF MY SURRENDERS

GUERNICA
EDITIONS

TORONTO—CHICAGO—BUFFALO—LANCASTER (U.K.)

2023

Guernica Founder: Antonio D'Alfonso

Michael Mirolla, general editor
Anna van Valkenburg, editor
Cover and Interior Design: Errol F. Richardson
Front cover image: Marc di Saverio
Guernica Editions Inc.
287 Templemead Drive, Hamilton (ON), Canada L8W 2W4
2250 Military Road, Tonawanda, N.Y. 14150-6000 U.S.A.
www.guernicaeditions.com

Distributors:
Independent Publishers Group (IPG)
600 North Pulaski Road, Chicago IL 60624
University of Toronto Press Distribution (UTP)
5201 Dufferin Street, Toronto (ON), Canada M3H 5T8
Gazelle Book Services
White Cross Mills, High Town, Lancaster LA1 4XS U.K.

First edition.
Printed in Canada.

Legal Deposit – Third Quarter
Library of Congress Control Number: 2022952298
Library and Archives Canada Cataloguing in Publication
Title: Songs of my surrenders / Marc di Saverio.
Names: Di Saverio, Marc, author.
Series: Essential poets ; 307.
Description: Series statement: Essential poets series ; 307 | Poems.
Identifiers: Canadiana 20230133282 | ISBN 9781771838511 (softcover)
Classification: LCC PS8607.I235 S66 2023 | DDC C811/.6—dc23

For Angela Macaluso... I proclaim:
without 'Angel', you cannot spell her name!

Contents

Part III

Part IV

Part V

Does the road wind up-hill all the way?
     Yes, to the very end.
Will the day's journey take the whole long day?
     From morn to night, my friend.
But is there for the night a resting-place?
     A roof for when the slow dark hours begin.
May not the darkness hide it from my face?
     You cannot miss that inn.
Shall I meet other wayfarers at night?
     Those who have gone before.
Then must I knock, or call when just in sight?
     They will not keep you standing at that door.
Shall I find comfort, travel-sore and weak?
     Of labour you shall find the sum.
Will there be beds for me and all who seek?
     Yea, beds for all who come.
                    —*Christina Rossetti (1830-1894)*

A NOTE ON THE TEXT

These poems were mainly penned between 2019 and 2021, and some were penned as early as 2006, then re-written or re-worked. Let it be known that I am an evolving Christian, and that I do not necessarily see eye to eye with all of the poems herein, but include them all for their artistic value, as markers of my own growth in the Spirit, and for other reasons not worthy of elucidation. For instance, you will notice that a few of the poems sound prophetic. Let it be known: I am NOT a prophet.

Warmly,
Marc di Saverio

PART I

Standing on Opposite Sides of The Stream Dividing the Ravine

for Paul di Saverio

Standing on opposite sides of the stream dividing the ravine—
   you singing verses and I singing choruses, then vice-versa;
   the spring stream thin; the kindred ravine dimming; mom
   biting her first nail on the phone with Aunt Josie; dad
   inside the study, reciting Leopardi; both at home.
Standing on opposite sides of the stream dividing the ravine—
   you practicing your curve-balls, I catching all your curve-
   balls; we synchronized brothers with same-sized shadows,
   equal in our gifts; the strongest want each having for the
   other being that the other would out-bloom, out-explode
   him, like one cherry-blossom might out-bloom, out-explode
   another—
Standing on opposite sides of the stream dividing the
   ravine—you praying to Saint Cecile, I praying to Saint
   Cecile; the cardinals, camouflaged by the late red rays,
   seeming to shoot out of nowhere, out of the vortex to the
   reason for coincidence, the Stranger's way of remaining
   anonymous?
And, soon, telling the time by the fainting sun, I'd jump
   the stream.
And, now, I remember that holy moment when we saw how
   beauteous it'd really be, to enter our paradisal home
   before our father—in his white undershirt, young still,
   glowing unlike the sun at the ends of those evenings—
   had set out toward us.

Ode to My Discoverer

for Jim Johnstone

Dare we, dare we, now, brotherly discoverer; dare our comet-
keenly spirits see through the narrow needle's eye seemingly
overlooking our paltry visions?
Dare we, now, dare we, mapless and guideless, see through
illusions of importance, which hang like densest fogs around a
Siamese light-house—dare we, then, finally voyage on feet-
bottoms so untraveled they're light-speedy, charged, charged,
charged enough to drive us on as, I envision, two off-white beams
of our eye-lights, shooting toward that unloosening eye, illuming,
suddenly, before us, a levitating bridge … and we'll wonder: Dare
we, dare we cross the hovering cobblestones like beggars do a street
toward a Salvation Army on the coldest night in fifty years?
Dare we, dare we, now, brotherly recoverer of my life,
lime-light-bringer-and-singer-for-moments, lime-light-blighter-and-
ouster-for-moments, wisely tired of fame before the fame is won?
Dare we, now, dare we burst forth like two myriad-mile darts of light
that beam toward the bullseye of the far-flung orbits of the Kingdom,
our target?
Dare we, now, dare we, brotherly discoverer, equally equipped, ramble,
march, crawl or even be carried toward a way no one goes for fear of
being blinded by disillusionment, which may or may not await them?
Dare we, dare we, now, forwarding with wonder, wondering with wisdom
gleaned in earlier times of our witnessing eyes, seeing to it that we
know which way to trail-blaze by simply finally beginning the universal
strut—charged, untraveled, mapless, but knowing the way, somehow?
Dare we, now, dare we?

I Dreamed a Game of Chess

I dreamed a game of chess wherein the white
side equalled the beast-mark deniers, the black
side equalled the beast-mark receivers—pieces
moved without a hand or string in sight. Two
sides, one humankind: those blinded by the dimmest
beams of Götterdämmerung, hunchbacked
in their engineered poltroonery, coin-
tossing their souls' indefinite future—their heirs'
fur coats hanging from hollow walking sticks—
the Last Generation of the West, and the First
Generation Of the Beast; and those whose braving
eyes project new truth-lights toward their down-
    cast kids—those whose white king, after feigning
    zugzwang, checks. On waking, white was reigning.

Song of a Seer to His Love

The Soldiers of the Lord—
       the Light Brigades of the Almighty—
   like snow melting from peaks,
  will run from mountaintops into the glades
         of blasted woods without one bloom.
Love, let's not be grim
      when the brownouts come—
        let's not reproof
our Fate but, rather, by dim candle-flames,
      dance to beats of raindrops on the roof
        accompanied by trumpets of the sky
played by measured winds of the Most High.

Orphaestus

… go, my songs, verse through the ears of the smilers-in-their sleep,
  bridge them to their wakes, sound both familiar as a tick when
  heard with a tock, and strange as the aura of   a living-room
  where a family along with CNN counts down the minutes of the
  last day on earth.
Go, too, my songs, blast the campers off the piggying back of great-
  great-great grandpa Dada.
Go to the poets skipping over the limbo bar of poetry;
Go, my songs, inspire the overthrow of phony poets professing to
  pliable neophytes. Behold: here is how to leap over poetry's limbo
  bar, and into the Antigonish.
Go, my songs, bridge an ephebic seer to his first awakening.
Go to the tear-skinned, wasp-cored souls that hang my off-shooting
  street; tell them if you have been granted equality, you have not
  received it.
Go to those fuck-stick rich kids cultivating an enviable ennui and
  reading campy pamphlets on how to become a heroin addict,
  cultivating cliches as ways and aim
to be properly impoverished …
Bring, sing, get morning bells to ring:
GOTTERDAMMERUNG! GOTTERDAMMERUNG!
while I the wise Mulciberian am still young …
Go like a closet-moth fluttering toward the sun …
Go my wannabe muses, transmute into muses …
Go through women who awaken aroused, who see their rosy breasts
  at dawn then fondle
    them then smile …

Go, knowing passion is vision and compassion is vision and the
     world's first incision; go, my songs, but try to try one world at a
     time ...
Go as a soft, psalmed, warm wind on my blood sister's spirit-lesion ...
Go too, songs, toward them, electrify both dance floors and psych
     wards.
Try to soothe the world-wide wound as blindly as heating bathwater
     would overflow the blobby or sculpturly body ...
Let the old recluse see sunset's red-salamander-cirrus.
Let your tyrant-torched melody lines re-vein Poetry.
Feel free to possess Ezra's tweed skeletons digging on the Island of the
     Dead because I only hear the splashing of his jewels in the sea ...
Go, you clubfooted songs; go in bulldozing throngs over America's
     rhetoric, then shroud it with sheets of its amateur anthems.
Cardiac-arrest the tyrant's rhetoricians, including myself, if I should
     become one.
Nerve-wrack all the tyrants with your by-produced seductiveness;
     inspire rioters to hang all the tyrants with slack.
Go, my songs: assassinate the assassins, then sing me and bring me
     their hit lists.
Go, my manic's afflatus:
no back-turn's wind will sweep the shardy stars,
no Agency will waste Nature's nurse,
no iron hand will bend your bars of verse.
Go, my songs, go whisperingly-singing to the silken souls of those
     who are hunch- backed in media.
Go, my songs, bitch in the voice of my brothers, sing in that
     of my fathers – go toward those who are feeling their ages or
     not, whirl in their bodies' wisdoms, then spin on the tops of
     your high notes then halt, in those who see we know they are
     broken—O peacekeepers in pieces, O hunchbacked-in-the-media,
     O so-deformed-unmockables, whose damages they nor I can

estimate, then hum for them softly when you are acquainted, tell
them you wish you could fix them with your presence.
Tell them you know a less fortunate boy, even if he does not exist;
tell them you know a less fortunate girl, a teenaging degenerate.
Go now me and mine through those I still am too proud to sleep
with.
Songs toward and through them all, but jive with what is sleepless.
Chorus in the souls of the hideously bodied.

2001, 2022

Summer Ku And Senryu

I
peeping star through rush of cloud—
lost on a trail through the myriad
ox-eye daisies

II
after the bonfire party ...
amid the slight light breeze,
moonlit milkweed-seeds float by

III
clear June afternoon—
over the flowerless graves,
shadows of the blue spruce rows

IV
hours after blackout ...
in one backyard, neighbours share the times they
first saw falling stars

V
shape-shifting clouds
before evening downpour—
breeze of flower-blends

VI
awakened by that nightmare—
the closet moth out-knocking my
firefly jar

VII
twilight—
as I strike my match, the fireflies
scatter

VIII

for Lenora Di Saverio

warm winds at the Mountain Brow—
for the first time since I was child I stop and sing to
the flowers

IX
the dew drops
unite, then tip
the fading iris

X
my father's 73rd—
like moths around the light of a lamppost, in the middle of the
    night,
we still all want to be around Him

XI
flow-tides after a bonfire-party—
though constellations fade toward the daybreak, in the rising sun's
    light, soon we will see the
bright white irises bloom

XII
     for Conor Mckeating

the light of a distant bonfire—
remember when, so young, we drove my blue Corolla insanely
    fast through the San Streets blasting Elastica's "Stutter"
that Summer?!

XIII
Pole Star …
school out for summer, the children of the children I used to hear
    laughingly splashing diagonally from my home's backyard—
    while I lay in bed, funereally hallucinating,   alone—
    compliment the drunken singing of my poetry, then race half
    a block—all the while we still conversing—to my backyard,
    so they can
meet me

XIV
entering Collevecchio…
through sheet lightning I can see
the room wherein my father was born

XV
more downpour—
amid the warm wind, a stranger welcomes me into her
veranda

XVI
the whitening clouds begin their clearing—
not the needles of the rain, nor the petal-rips from blasting winds,
    nor the loss of entire capitula, will shake the wild
white irises of their glory

XVII
eve of Canada Day—
at Nelligan's tomb, the goths
lay down their lilies

XVIII
the galaxies …
how will I find a life partner who will leave me alone for
most of the time?

XIX
suchness—
my blue irises bloom behind their gray morning housecoats
of fog

XX

the flash of twilight fireflies …
at the end of the long ravine
the blaze of night's white stars

XXI
the blooming white irises ...
in the Sanatorium courtyard
no one delights

Sonnet XII

for Diane Windsor

No, O no, the evil envy
of those lesser lookers in
your life—those ones who fun-housed every
looking glass you've ever glanced—
shall not triumph since, until
you see your beauty at last, I
will be your mirror. And till you cry
your final, flimflam-fleeing tear
at last, I'll not stop reflecting
Pygmalion's Galatea,
if ever she still lived; reflecting
the fairest proportions, causing the dour
distortions of your enviers.
Yes, O yes, I'll be your mirror.

Pygmalion

for Jim Johnstone

Though King of Cyprus, I so only wish to rule my hands,
not Cypriots; to manage marble, not
unrest; to command statues, not soldiers! Who stands
alone so dawn-sun-dazzlingly as the statues of Cypriots
over-populating my palace?! Lately,
fathoming the whoredom of the Prop-
oetides, my mid-summer-swimmingly lust, lightning
forthwith, drowned in waste-land-waters of
my disgust! No beauty queen of Cyprus
ever matches my yet-to-be chiselled, only-ever-
in-dreams appearing, uttermost woman—
Galatea—whom I now free from marble
whiter than the midnight moonlight paling upon her. It does not help
that my tastes are refined to a fault. By dawn my Gala-
tea will be one's-last-breath-completed,
will be universe-perfected. Though King of Cyprus, I
am pole-star single; might Aphrodite
animate my dream woman of stone,
so I may fall in first-and-last love? Though King
of Cyprus, I can't fall for any living
woman… Now, dawn, fall for this one breathing statue.
"My king, my king, behold me: I am Galatea."
To kings so only wishing for their lonesome-
ness's end: hold no dominions over
any apexes—it is only lonely at the top
for those who will not share their higher ground with others.
My queen, my queen, please hold me: I'm Pygmalion!

PART II

The Villanelle of Carmello D. Chiulla

Although my hand is guided by the hand of God—
although I am the voice of one who's crying in the wilderness—
O do not marvel at me, my free hand is flawed;

marvel at my Maker—marvel at His unshod
King of Kings whose wound-beams bless forth life-end tunnel-lights for us.
Although my hand is guided by the hand of God,

do rival palms hold fit to prayer-press? Am I a fraud
or, like Moses and others, do I speak His words and yet transgress?
O do not marvel at me, my free hand is flawed

and offends me, and offends us; should my free hand be sawed,
to set sail my ported soul, anchored by my sin-stress?
Although my hand is guided by the hand of God,

marvel at the model Christ; to be jaw-dropped and awed
by me, while reading the Almighty's verses, is blasphemy? Yes!
O do not marvel at me; my free hand is flawed!

O pray for my perfecting, reader, and never laud
me; laurel the head of the Lord, alone, so my soul may progress.
Although my hand is guided by the hand of God,
O do not marvel at me; my free hand is flawed.

Sonnet of Impending Ending

I see, while teased by flower blends in a breeze,
it's true: when we were one I could not dream
since you were all of my expectancies
arriving like this late summer moonbeam
on your body, which my eye no longer sees
as an astronomer sees the universe.
Remember when my soul lifted your curse?
When eye-lights of your blisses would high-beam
upon the earth? The balm of my tenure was hard
as death to summon and, though love died, this bard—
between sleeping and waking—feels we are one
again; though we doze through nights without one
touch. I live for times I think we're still one stream—
for times I wake and still am in a dream.

Sonnet XIII

for Diane Windsor

Even the time I spend apart from you
is yours. Even scarcely tenable
quavers of your smiles are seen to *the*
whole world inside my electric soul;
even the memory of your voice's lower-
most echo blasts away any noises, accompan-
ies me through the loneliest, hollow silences.
Even your Galatean shadow is bodied—and souled—
in my heart. Even the time I spend apart
from you is yours. Even others with
your name are more forgivable
to me. Even Angels of the Light
discuss us, I believe. Even
awake beside you sleeping, I cannot dream.

When I Was Still the Husband of The Wind

for Diane Windsor

When I was still the husband of the wind—
when I was Leopardi-sure I'd never
know a woman's body's ways—when I
was nineteen and Prufrock-positive
of mermaids never singing to me,
of a life without betrothal or progeny;
when I was one of the hideously-bodied;
When I was still the husband of the wind—
I would dream, like Pygmalion, of my donna perfetta.
One whose soul was as beauteous as her body,
One whose nature was sublime but unlikely.
I would dream that she would come to life,
that she would meet me at the brow, and love me. And, now,
beside you, awake while you sleep, I see: she is you.

Autumn Ku

I
blown from its bough
an oak's last leaf now
darts: a cardinal!

II
returning from the bar ...
also bumbling and desolate
a late October wasp

III
recess ...
the same old janitor drops fall's roofed balls, one by one,
to roars of his clamourers

IV

    for Marco Pecora

the Mountain Brow ...
the horizon-line smiles the way you would when you'd find
    another spider for your mason jar those nights when, as boys,
    we'd smoke till dawn on that toy boat the size of a veritable
    ship—down at
the Hamilton Harbour

Whisperingly, Whimperingly Singing to Me, Blind

for Lenora Di Saverio

Whisperingly, whimperingly singing to me, blind,
through the lightless halls of stifled air,
you lock yourself in the mausoleum of my mind

where ethereal steps depress a shifting floor of signed-
away dreams, graven in fears, which double-dare.
Whisperingly, whimperingly singing to me, blind,

among the screams of live-tombed hopes in walls aligned
with the bruising echoes of my exploding tear,
you lock yourself in the mausoleum of my mind

where, blighted by my past clock's self-wind
you're reborn in your nowing force to share,
whisperingly, whimperingly singing to me, blind.

Wasped in spite you whip your arm and the wind
you break waves a moment's light of your halo-sheer care.
You lock yourself in the mausoleum of my mind,

my breath-broken mother, ungravely given to maligned
mourning draughts of nada's laughing eye-pinning stare.
Whisperingly, whimperingly singing to me, blind,
you lock yourself in the mausoleum of my mind.

A Translation of Arthur Rimbaud's "Le Mal"

While the crimson spittle of the grapeshot
whistles all day through the deathless blue skies;
while, near the jeering King, green or scarlet
soldiers fall, en masse, in a fire, with cries!

While a ghastly madness grinds a hundred
thousand men into a steaming pile—poor dead
men among the long summer grass-blades!
Nature, O you who turn these men to saints!

He's a God who mocks the frankincense and myrrh,
the damask tablecloths, the gold altar—
a God who's rocked to sleep by hosannas,

who's awakened by mothers united in throes,
weeping and screaming in their old black hats,
giving Him pennies bound in their handkerchiefs.

A Translation of Émile Nelligan's "Winter Sentiments"

for Diane Windsor

So now I drink the liquors of your eyes!
Don't soil yourself while gazing at the masses!
A blast from Norway turns the fields to steel!
May hearts turn warm when the cold wind passes!

Like soldiers mourning level sands at Thebes
so let us always court our rancours
and, despising life, with its sophistic song,
let Death lead us to Orcus, where we belong.

You'll visit like an icy spectre; we won't be old,
but already so weary of living we will fold;
O Death, take us out on such an afternoon

when I'm etherized by my lover's guitars,
whose dreamy motifs and ambient bars
keep time to our ennui on the waltz to the end!

A Translation of Arthur Rimbaud's "Au Cabaret Vert"

After one week of the road-stones ripping my
boots to shreds, Charleroi,
where I ordered some bread at the Cabaret-
Vert—and butter, and half-chilled ham—and, happy,

I stretched my legs out beneath a green table,
I gazed into the basic tapestries—
and O, it was exquisite, when the girl
with lovely boobs and lively eyes,

—she's never one to stiffen when she's kissed—
laughing, brought me bread and butter
and tepid ham on a florid dish,

ham that was garlic-scented, white and rose—
and filled my giant mug with beer
whose suds an evening beam turned gold.

I Shall Not Have It Such That You Should Sigh

for Carlo Di Saverio

I shall not have it such that you should sigh
every time we must speak of the future.
I shall not have it such that you would lie
on your deathbed; I in catatonic stupor
one room over, where I have been sleeping
since I spirit-soaringly dreamt of being
a whole man—my heart then beating inside a whole boy
with the health of a demi-god. A whole boy.
Though souls exceed themselves throughout their sorrows,
Joy's dew must be sipped to prosper tomorrows.
Considering my life after yours yields
"must stop like wilful sin," your spirits cry!
How could I have it such that you would die
Considering the lilies of the fields?!

A Sonnet to the Reader

   Do you taste the dusty airs of Orcus
when you're struck by a breeze of flower-blends?
   Do you feel the fleering stares of the circus
when you wait for a bus while the sun ascends?—
   A circus held in Hell by live incisions?
   Do you overlook the Bible's visions?
Some read His words as jewellers do their jewels.
Some read His words as foolers do their fools.
   Some read His words like throwing-stones at a wall
   where sinners wait to die without a stall.
O reader of His stepping-stones, I'm lonely—
   O reader of my spirit's fever, do I
question you for naught? Am I the only
   one who hears the trumpeters of the sky?

PART III

A Translation of Émile Nelligan's "And the Leaves Were Still Falling"

for Diane Windsor

I

The Angelus was sounding and the boy was atrociously pained to his bed—barely fifteen—the cold raving winds only adding to his anguish. But his mother, lamenting at the foot of his bed, saddened him even more, pained him further. Suddenly, joining his pale hands in heavenly prayer, and resting his nearly lifeless eyes on the crucifix, he made a sweet humble prayer which ascended to heaven like a delicate fragrance. And outside, in the cold night, the faint sounds of the bell of the small nearby church rose mournfully as they seemed, in advance, to toll the death knell of the young invalid. The cottage, lost in the countryside, was sheltered by tall poplar trees concealing it from the distance. In that place, beautiful blue mountains were on display, one by one, but they now seemed rather black because the horizon was becoming darker and darker.

II

The birds in the groves no longer sing, and all these songbirds which had once enlivened spring and summer had now flown away to unknown places. The leaves are falling and the autumn breeze whines in the branches; it is dark outside; but these sorrows of nature, these prolonged moans of the wind, are nothing more than the distant echoes of this immense pain that is keeping watch at the bedside of the patient whom God is asking back from the mother …

The old clock in the cottage sounds eleven; the boy has just beckoned to come even closer to the one who has lavished her attention upon him during many days and nights. She gets near, weakening, and listens carefully to the words that the dying boy whispers to her ear with great difficulty. "Mother," he says, "I'm going away … but I will not forget you up … there … where … I hope … to see you again one day … don't cry … come close for one last time to the crucifix at my lips … since I have only a few moments to live … goodbye dear mother … you know the place where I used to sit last summer … under the big oak tree … well, it's there … where I wish … to be … buried … Goodbye mom; take heart." The mother does not cry; like Mary at the foot of Calvary, she embraces her cross … suffers … and generously makes her sacrifice … Meanwhile the leaves are still falling; the ground is littered with these omens that are at the same time tragic and mournful; in the cottage the silence is solemn, the lamp emits in the funerary room a funereal faint glimmer that projects itself on the white face of the scarcely cold body, the window is completely wet by nightly spindrift, and the wailing breeze continues to make mournful sounds in the glades. Alas! The youth of the young patient has vanished like the flower of the fields that dies, for want of water, under the scorching rays of the shining sun.

How nature, the woods, the trees, the valley seemed sad that day, for it was autumn … and the leaves were still falling.

My Tears Now Flood and Skew

for Diane Windsor

My tears now flood and skew the few
blue words sigh-sailing this gray and rippling
page into obscurity
while I, memorizing these shades
of verse before they're cried away,
founder in my curse of life
without you. A wind of dust
blows my tears into the daisies
of the jetty where I wait
for you continuously; is
it true, what they say, that you
no longer—no longer
love me? I will wait
here, still. I will not move.

2010's, 2022

Though Broken I Must Sing the Verve of Earth

for Diane Windsor

Though broken I must sing the verve of earth
And though solo I must cheerlead lovers
To epiphanies of ecstasy under their covers,
Where both forget me like one does one's birth.
Though shattered I must mirror the whole, whose worth
Vision-sleeves the future and four-leaf clovers,
The daisy-dieted aimless rovers
Of slithering streets in the starlight.
No mirth in me, but I must laugh a lecture at the joke
Of society; and though my eye-light splits the sunbeams,
I must praise the Nature that broke
My body. Though hopeless I must truth their dreams.
Though my slaving veins do strangle me slowly,
I still sing you, Di, though you won't hold me.

2010's, 2022

A Two-Hundred-Year-Old Tenzone

for Jason Guriel

i. A Translation of Giacomo Leopardi's "Alla Luna"

O graziosa luna, I remember how
I dolorously climbed this hill to gaze
on you a year ago now, and, looming
over the forest there, which you illumed
then as you illume now, your visage
seemed, in my view, veiled and shaking
because of tears that twinkled on my eye-
lashes—my life was full of throes, and, still,
is unchangeable, O my beloved
moon—and it pleases me to precisely
recall the season of my suffering.
How sweet it is to remember the time
of youth, when the road of hope's still long
and that of memory short, to call
to mind the things of the past, even though
they're sad, and the agony lives on!

1820

ii. A Dream of Natura

I feel Her sea-sky lips' horizon kiss!
Step-mother Nature must love me, today!
For a while I'll be wind-blown toward my bliss
with flowers full-bowing to me on my way,

through romance unforgettable as death,
through woods with airs of paradisal traces,
through talks of gold with the cliffside-faces,
which only respond to her favourites;
yet I have also felt Step Mother prick
me, like a sacrificial baby, with stinging
February winds. Will I be on
this way, tomorrow? The sail of my soul
is so full of gales that its pirates quite drown
in its wake while it rides, as my eyes open.

2020

This Newly Ever-Rising Freshwater of All Your Love

for Diane Windsor

This newly ever-rising freshwater of all your love,
  is dammed by ever-rising stones, each mortared
     by wearying poltergeists and all your dying distrust
     since, no greater love can a man have than this:
Than to lay down his life for his friend; for you I have laid down
     my life—
        and I know you know I would lay it again.
        By the aegis of the Lord I outlived my own
sacrifice, and because you can see me, still, hear me, still, touch
Me, still—how unique to know the man who prayed "O help
     me to die
like a lion, even if I am a lamb." The King of Kings has worked
His miracle of life for you to trust—a miracle
Because, before reborn in the Spirit, before transformed by the Holy
Ghost, I was so unjust to you. Beside the Heavenward dam, deserted,
I need your new waters; yet for now, I'll live on all the tears of
how I wronged you.

A Translation Of Émile Nelligan's "The Black Cloister"

They step in time to the tread of their sandals—
praying heavy beads with their heads bowed—
and the blood-reflecting evening heavens
bronze the flagstones' funereal glory.

They soon withdraw, like in shady mazes,
down passages of purple relays,
where angels of the stained-glass windows
ban the earthly scandals' entry.

Their faces are dismal, and in their eyes
like vast horizons of maritime skies
there blazes the austerity of ways I've seen.

A divine light fills their universal minds
since a winning hope now finally finds
these silent spectres of the Nazarene.

Am I the Lone One Who Dreams of the Other

Am I the lone one who dreams of the other
so exhaustively the other is dreamed
into being, we uniting, once more, like
drying brooks into one stream? Or,
have your memories of me been drowned
inside the sea of your abashment of us—been lapsed
in another's love, not conditionless
like mine, but one considered most becoming
of our times? Am I the lone one who dreams
to dispute the truth of this life without the other?
Over stable stepping-stones of my own
life, you trampled toward salvation. Now you're
wife and mother, as prescribed—and what am I
but some sunless stairway you stamped to the sky?

A Sonnet on Ephesians 5:25

for Diane Windsor

And how you modern readers wonder why I call her thee?
It is because you've never seen or known her apogee.

And at the crucifixion-slow-mo-mentioning
of me and you, the lovers of future Valentine's
Days will wonder, Romeo and who? No greater
love can a man have than this: than to lay down his life for his friend;
No greater love can a man have than mine; for you I laid
down my life, and for you I'd lay it again—able by
the aegis of the Lord, without whom I would be gone …
        If I did not, if I do not, if I
        would not so strive to love you just as Jesus
        loves His Bride, I'd flee from thee as the Devil
        fled the moment after he thirdly sought
        to tempt I AM. Calvary's my only
        guide to loving thee, so my heart beats
        Di-ane, Di-ane, Di-ane, Di-ane, Di-ane.

The Sonnet of Luca Dulino

Canada, I came to you with my soul
and with diamonds, and you tried to collapse them
back into a vacuum, back into coal!—
Canada, remove your bloody diadem!
Canada, I came to you with answers
to inquiries you make in your lion-wild
dreams, where your wonder has been exiled,
where your wishes are kites so drawn to stirs
of the vortex of utopia, through
whose one end I blow, as though through a trumpet,
the prophecies you mock, despite sensing,
deep in your soul's centre—you freeze—
the chance my drawn and quartered words are true,
these testaments to my theophanies!

A Translation of Leopardi's "L'infinito"

All along I loved this lonely knoll
and this horizon-eclipsing hedgerow
excluding most my view.
Sitting and staring, my mind strays into
the interminable spaces of superhuman
silence, of quietest quiet, and so
my heart's fear nearly fades away—
and as I hear the gust
rustling among the shrubs, I liken this voice
to that infinite silence. Then I remember
the everlasting, past ages;
the incessancy of the present—
the din of it; and thus
my thought is drowned in this immensity,
and wrecks of such seas are so sweet to me.

A Translation of Arthur Rimbaud's "Voyelles," Version Two

for Diane Windsor

A noir, E blanc, I rouge, U vert, O bleu: voyelles,
some day your secret pregnancies I'll tell:
A, black corset of blazing hairy
flies that buzz above a nasty

funk, bays of shade; E, steams
and tents' naivety—white kings, haughty glacial spears,
shadows shivering; I, crimsons, bloodspit, lovely lips
that laugh in wrath or repentant drunkenness;

U, cycles, viridian seas divine vibrations,
peace of cattle-scattered pastures, peace
of wrinkles which alchemy imprints on the high and the studious

brows; O virginal stridors of Trumpet Supreme,
Silences diagonal with Angels and Realms—
O, L'Omega, His Eyes' violet beam!

PART IV

Sonnet to the Bride of Christ

for Christopher Galano

The Bride of Christ—we who'll die uncaptured
by the System of the Beast, we arrested-
in-body-but-not-in-spirit—unrested,
in camps, will dream of being raptured
while our whippers are most wrathful—the Word
our credence's diamond armour. Not bested
by the Beast, we will be, for Christ, tested
and tested to take the Mark, yet, cured
of lusts for our own Hours of Shadows,
cured of lusts to save our flesh from throes!—
by the Holy Ghost—We, the Bride, entrust
in Christ whose strides do break the gale which blows
the trumpets of prophecies. While bleeding we must
recall: the Blood of the Lamb will not mingle with dust.

A Translation of Charles Baudelaire's "Gypsies' Journey"

for Christopher Galano

Last night this tribe of fiery-eyed foreseers
set out on its way again with mothers
back-bearing babies who when hungry shed no tear
'cause treasure-breasts are always hanging near.

On foot these men go under gleaming weapons—
while their own lie inside nearby wagons—
and cast over skies with their leaden-lidded eyes
that grimly regret the absent chimeras.

From the heart of his sandy hole the cricket, seeing
them pass, redoubles his singing;
and Cybele, who loves them so, makes more of her

greenery, turns the rocks to streams that rush, flowers
the deserts ahead of these roamers free to endure
their familiar empire's gloomy future.

O To Never See My Highest Deeds of Love Felt In Your Heart

for Diane Windsor

O to never see my highest deeds of love felt in your heart;
O to never see my highest offerings known in your soul—
These are the nightmares from which I must awaken, so we will hold,
inside where sorrow so carved into our union, a virgin joy.
O to never see my love explode into the widest smile
ever seen upon your face, before our first new-born embrace.
All my feats and sacrifices of one fulsome year,
the very ones you'd once not ever dare to dream would ever be
to you, from me, have lain in your mind like unknown soldiers under
the dusts of your inner blind-eye-turns, rather than have waterfallen
through your thirstingly existing heart. Besides my Salvation,
my wish of wishes is for you to know, by my love, a new value.
Where still my screaming essence bleeds in a black spasmodic fit,
now open your eyes to our love, Diane, or close All Time on it.

Winter Ku And Senryu

I
first snow—
a half-drawn nude is
rubbed from the window

II
the woman lets me in
this rush hour—
light snow

III
through the high narrow hall
of cliff-side and frozen waterfall,
coo-ah-coo coo-coo

IV
why did I blaze this trail?
snow clouds gather in
the dusk

V
the pre-dawn snowstorm departs—
a couple strides, then sprints, then slides
down the middle of Main Street

VI

for Conor Mckeating

the violet sky—
a street-light flickers on, in the dusk, the snow so bright it
looks like dawn

VII

walking through the storm, alone—
a whirlwind of snow reminds me of times we danced together as
children

VIII

Mount Fuji—
it is only lonely at the top for those who will not share their
        higher ground
with others

IX

spring is near …
a homeless man blows a smoke-ring through another,
then another over both, yet, unlike me, is not in awe

X

Christmas Eve …
I approach, with an unlit cigarette,
the bag-lady blowing thick rings of breath

A Translation of Gérard de Nerval's "Golden Verses"

Freely thinking man, so, you think only you can
have a thought on earth where verve is bursting
inside everything, you with the forces and freedom
˙to command a cosmos absent while you plan?!

Revere the spirit inside the insect! Man,
know each flower's a soul that faces up to our
one Mother at dawn, know all metals repress
mysteries of love. All things feel! And all's in your power!

Watch out: in walls without eyes are the glances of spies;
any matter has a verb attached;
do not use it impiously.

Hiding deities often dwell inside the vaguest beings,
and like a newborn's eye still sealed,
the pure soul flowers underneath stone peel.

May The Sonnet Be My Second Currency?

for Diane Windsor

May the sonnet be my second currency?
Although I have no fund, I own this form.
Your love next to the love of other ladies
is like the polestar next to other stars. While storm
-wind-wild as flapless soaring mourning doves, we
sip the pinecone dew and watch the firefly jars.
While blitheful as the soul is real as the Devil,
we're forthcoming as our breaths, real as Gabriel
(to whom we pray for further revelations—
who answers us in flickers of star-equations).
Your love next to the love of other ladies
is like a breeze of flower-blends next to other breezes;
I'm faithful as a mirror framed and set in densest stone
because you measure my worth by my love, alone.

Because My Heart So Naturally Darts

Because my heart so naturally darts for the tear-skinned
wasp-cored souls that hang my off-shooting street,
now I must crib my heart in bars of verse, and retreat
into this virginal wood, and know You will not think I've sinned.
Yet bars of verse can only hold until my thought is turned;
they bow for You and your souls out-discerned.
Love I naturally cannot find, yet none can none my love;
yet my retreating heart, like this cardinal bleeding
in the claws of a black-hawk, is still beating—
in my mental grip—for the realm it must rise above.
Still whimperingly singing, still carelessly unknowing,
it can but camouflage its blood by showing;
still faintfully ascending, now, the high and kinless brow,
to feed a bald and tweetless brood, who knows no bird below.

The Man with The Micro-Chip in His Right Hand

Stopping wantless under cherry blossoms,
He hears a girl singing from the sewer,
then harmonizes voices with some hums,
then sings the final chorus like he knows her,
their voices shaking red chrysanthemums—
but now the crowds of fading stars are fewer
and his voice grows weaker as the day glows nearer,
as he's alarmed by the stirrings of the bums.
"Should I come up to see you on the street
so in the morning light we could now meet?"
A blossom plummets through the dewy grate.
Before he can reply I, an old class-mate,
pass by, asking why he's standing here—
"for—for cherry-trees this time of year."

PART V

Since I Cannot Undrop Your Tears That Innocently Fell

for Diane Windsor

Since I cannot undrop your tears that innocently fell
      like one, same, sightless girl, over and over,
into a well—whenever you're out watching comedies
with Kim, I weep, at home, inside my bed, again and again.
Since I cannot unfeel your fears that reasonably seized
      you like a city through a war—your fears of girls
my age—whenever you're out overrunning Hamilton
on hikes, I restitute my best for you with melodies like these.
      At last you've known the virgin joy of our
      newborn embrace. At last you know you hold
      a man you once believed an immortal boy.
      At last you know this hold shall never cease,
      yet since those years were lost to me in scores,
      even my time apart from you is yours.

A Sonnet After a Winter Surrender

O Seraph who stands on sacred airs—
goldening the firmament with halo-
beams—illumining my soul with
rosary-stars, which supernova
after your Amens; you whisperingly singing
over me, soaring my soul like a whitening kite
triple-tied to an infinite string…
O Seraph who lands on burn-out back-
yards of this downcast world, when
will this tempest end?! "Know: I only
seem a Seraph! I am come,
tonight, to witness your rebirth!
Revere the spirit inside the whiteout;
the snow foreshadows my Kingdom on Earth!"

A Sonnet for My Father

for Carlo Di Saverio

It is raining birds in Italy!
   Stiff starlings bestrew the streets like black
roses on those graves of her cities! A funereal
   waltz wails through the Colosseo. Crack-
smoke wafts through ancient olive groves. Verily,
   the Roman Forum is now bric-a-brac
standing 'round like extras on a film-set,
considering the End, my father; and, yet,
   pentameters re-pace my heart, which beats—
adrenalized with memories—for your home,
   where once the Beast-barons had no drums nor fleets—
(our days turned to weeks like water to foam)—
      where once we dreamed, back-to-back, in the bed where you
      were born—where once each sight was one's best view.

Fragment For a Heaven-Farer

for Diane Windsor

According to that Acolyte who lived to see His Second Coming
(circa 66-70)—
no greater love can a man have than this—
than to lay down his life for his friend;
According to the Acolyte who lived to see the Gallops of Glory
(within that single generation)—
no greater love can a man have than mine—
I'm warming outside James Street storefronts where once
our sea-sky lips would,
stunning passers-by, horizon their romance-less eyes with
each of our own perfect kisses;
I'm slumming throughout air-stung hoar-frosts where once
our sea-sky lids would,
shunning passers-by, thunderclap their romance-less hearts with
each of our own perfect visions;
Yet, take thought: the adversary's maximum extensions are harpoons
he swears are darts of amities knee-
jerkingly flung automatically as beams toward their
midnight moons, or smiles of mothers
whose conditionless love so helplessly blooms in the faces
of red-eyed teens all synch-ly slouching at their court hearing.
I surmise The Devil has not heard, and I hope, Diane, you'll finally know:
calm can only come by the one called
that violet-eye-light-beaming Jesus Christ—
and Lucifer, like a late-autumn wasp with stinging wings
frosting in the twilight, KNOWS his death is near,
so he quavers in fright, privately, yet publicly,
jabs a maximum of souls, which he considers his birthright;

And, take thought: I often wonder If you,
                 yes, Job-long-suffering you, weeping-willow-boughs
-amid-the-winter-wind-unassuming you, ever
         owned the value to wonder: Might I be one to write as
                       fast as the Almighty
speaks, might I be the Stenographer of the Lord, never even needing
              any breaks (O Lucifer, YOU believe
                that you will beat her hand at any sort
       of duel? Her hand is guided by the hand of God! O Lucifer,
          she is ready!) So, Di, when you face him, Eastwood-easy,
                      DRAW!
And, take thought: the force that drives my spirit drives your own,
                yet the spirit of Satan dives
like Iscariot dove from the rope-ripped-bough throughout the Hour
                    Of Shadows. Remember,
Satan—regardless of his wishes, despite being SMALL-g god of this
          World—is merely the prop-foil-prelude
             secondary to so many myriad dualities created by
The Trinity, his eventual Bermuda Triangle. Until his disappearance,
            he is the mere adversary,
              the one alone the Lord esteems enough
       to consider His clearest, but maybe not His most fearsome, opponent;
              who has darkness both behind and before
     him! So how, Diane, is he even a Light-Bearer,
           since, wherefrom comes his light? He KNOWS
         he is finite—he worships the finite, so how can he be
bright—especially in the face of your light, woman-of-my-dreams-
     and-of-the-dreams-within-my-dreams?

Portrait of The Artist as His Prints on The Walls

I rotate the picture frames monthly; today
Man Ray's "Masks" are watching over my bed,
And Picasso's "Girl With Mandolin"
Is strumming before his "Harlequin
With Companion," half-facing her.
Over the rocking chair:
Max Ernst's "Forest."
Behind my desk is
Goyo's "Snow At Mount Ibuki,"
Always falling.

And facing me,
Dali's "Cosmic Athlete"
Clutching the sun, as though it were a discus;
With winding stairs going 'round his feet, through
His heel and up to his head, with one foot in pivot;
In stance to launch his light over all
The skies and soils, over
Highest gods and pantheons,
Over rulers and battles and blood,
The Eastern Aqueducts.

Spring Haiku and Senryu

I
first rain—
all these finger-graven flowers in
the snow

II
Easter Dawn—
the closet moth defenestrates, then flutters toward
the sun

III

ice-bound waters in the floes—
flapping and gliding my memory
blue-winged butterflies

IV

     for Lenora Di Saverio

the warm wind—
like fists upholding hilts of swords before a queen, the snows are
     upholding last year's iris-shoots before
You, mother

V
I wander,
drunk, through an abandoned off-shoot street, lost—
the thunder

VI

for Lenora Di Saverio

the warm, Mother's Day wind—
so high am I from all the love you give, that, while I wonder if
      one's glow alone might heal another's heart, I scrape my
      legs against the sidewalk pavement like high-rises that
      scrape against
the spring dawn sky

VII

for Martin Verral

the composition is really
the wind through the chimes—
the scent of a lily

VIII

warm spring winds through James Street North—
even the old Italian men are watching the
midnight street-fight

IX

sunrise—
like the iris-blooms weighed down by the dewdrops, her spirits are
low

X

the wheel-chaired child smiles
while her mother pushes her through
the wild mountain roses

XI
across the pitch-dark park
a couple runs and sings through the spring's
first lightning

XII. *Translation of Shiki*

a fallen blossom
flies back to its stem—
A butterfly!

XIII
a cocoon becomes the monarch butterfly
the way a wind through the verdure becomes the wind through
her hair

XIV
twilight—
after having swum since dawn, with each oncoming tide, the
        Adriatic Sea
waves at me

Aube

Once upon a sanatorium stay
I dreamed love beamed where no light shone
while rain washed no hard crow-dung away
from the Nelligan statue toppled in the dawn.
I could not lift my brother from the lawn
so I rubbed the dung from his eyes as I lay
beside the bronze bard who knelt to pray
for me a century ago: after I am gone,
another one will rave throughout these grounds.
O Lord, that you might spare him of my fate!
I peeled the worm from between his lips.
Late that morning I woke to what still astounds
me to tears. Nelligan singing in my ear:
This will be the last voix fausse you'll hear!

———————————

Jesus the Redeemer Singles Out a Dancer At The Jubilee of the Second Coming

for Lenora Di Saverio

Lone among the dancers, you mourn—despite Death's adieu—
my Calvary anew, behind your sunglasses?
Woman, none stands alone so beautifully as you,

since, has the Kingdom not Come? You say your tears are dew?
Why now cry amid the trumpets and the brasses?!
Lone among the dancers, you mourn, despite Death's adieu—

Mourn the dead Inferno-hours of the Risen Son, too?
O won't you jive and join in chalice-clangs?
Woman, none stands alone so beautifully as you.

Why should you not waltz to a flawless few
Of Cecile's tunes? Whiff this lilied wind that passes?
Lone among the dancers, you mourn, despite Death's adieu.

I feel no sorrow; must my whippings ensue?
Should you not see family, upon my greenest grasses?
Woman, none stands alone so beautifully as you.

Behold the tear-toning stars! Behold your halo-hue
supremely match my moon! To Lea, raise your glasses!
Lone among the dancers, she mourns, despite Death's adieu—
Woman, none stands alone so beautifully as you.

Awaiting the Knocks of the Devil's Assassins; Awaiting

dedicated to Kelley Lewis

Awaiting the knocks of the devil's assassins; awaiting
our nation's techno-medical martial
law; awaiting next new wool-white thoughts of our partial
Maker; awaiting the devil's temptations and baiting;
awaiting betrayals by neighbours with whom we traded
keys; awaiting to fight till each tear of the fallen un-drips;
awaiting snake-fang-sinkings of forced needle-tips;
awaiting the Second Coming—and still uninvaded—
we soldiers of the Lord, we Light Brigades
of The Almighty, flock to Flatrock amid house-raids
and curfewed men's cries for wives defiled by unbeckoned
mercenaries. Womb-kicked-seeming snow-clouds birth
these peace-delivering powder-drops, and, for a second,
it seems the Kingdom of Heaven is falling to earth.

The Lovesong of J & C

for Justin D'Amico

"We see you, you mother's-peekaboos-merest spies—
We hear you, you gang-stalkers in the still midnight.
O wish-washers, YOU target US, you bull-talkers?!
Our Holy-Ghost-ridden glimpse-rays never miss your bulls' eyes.
How will you skeletons of Satan's closet-suite
'terrorize' us? Don't you see we stride with seven armoured
Seraphim, whose match, like femmes, you'll never meet
(unless for hire), you push-overs upon the cliff's edge
of our utmost Faith—Faith force-fields us—but sure, attack!
You might as well be punching marble statues. How will you crack
us up, you father's-tuck-ins-never-disturbing nicest tries!
Why do you still follow us, you spirit-hawkers—
you black-hole-lightless hell-bound hounds—you trolls
will be blinked away by the eyes of our souls!"

Stay! —No, Go, Go; How Can You Leave Me, Now

Stay!—no, go, go; how can you leave me now
I've already so expressly finger-
snap-fastly saved you from your own hands,
then treated you like a heritage site?! I,
now, too, need deliverance, from you,
or else my thought-line will soon be
one long wound until the end
of my funeral-danceless life, whose marrow
is inside you. Now music is merely
a sound—a painting is simply a sight.
Why must I feel the full circle of my life
in my prime—in this last-like moment?!
What more could anyone have done for you?
Go! —no, stay, stay; how can you leave me, how?!

2006, 2021

The Oohs and Coos of Mourning Doves Still Soothe

The oohs and coos of mourning doves still soothe—
yet not as your laughter's lowermost echoes,
yet not as your spirit's dimmest afterglows.
You, despite my saving you with my own hands—
You, despite my saving you from your own hands—
forsake me now when I need you to save me?! Smooth.
I'm blind from after-flashes true love casts
the moment lovers rive forevermore.
Did you really jeer me, calling me a dreamer?
Those without dreams are like ships without masts—
You blinked our memories into our pasts,
yet when you sleep you will see me, you schemer.
Forgiving you shall be this fool's last will,
yet would you even go to my funeral?

2006, 2021

I Would Weep Your Tears and Mourn

for Paul di Saverio

I would weep your tears and mourn
your errors, I would live your nightmares
and feel your terrors; I would taste
the wastelanding waters of your soul

if I could only see your eyes
sunrise-serene, again, could only
see you wear a world-wide smile.
To see your return, I would live out

your exile. I will not dance
until, again, you play your aurora
borealis violin.

I will not dance until you sing;
I will not dance with any other.
I would die your death for you, my brother!

2021

Ode to the Moment Our Eyes First Locked (MMVI)

That time our eyes first locked, I swear I saw
in your starless, moonless soul, night-to-day-turning
steady-striking-yellow-vipers-seeming lightning
illumining wasteland-dust-dunes, while a raw
neon sewage slithered through the level sands
and whereon both sides of a soaring, stringless,
lonely kite, two paintings—two portraits, stroke by stroke,
one of you and one of me—materialized, over no town-folk,
over badlands we'd full-flower with our infinite bliss-blossoms.
O what is there to dream if you lie next to me, dreamless?
O what is there to see if you are in my sight, seamless?
That time our eyes first locked me in your life
you swore you saw, in my soul, oases.
With you all prisons are fair as your skin, my to-be wife!

2006, 2022

MARC DI SAVERIO

Ode to the Mountain Brow

dedicated to Richard Greene

Cliff-topped at dawn in a euphoria so high
I Paradise-verily see your wan white Pisa-
Towering streetlights well-tipping utmost fealty
to me, one I electrify back toward
you with this Ode I compose under cadaver-
soullessly blackening clouds—streetlights well-tipping
with dew-new currency of gray-brown fogs and truth-
pellucid allusions to Expressionist movies I adore.
Now, forthwith, I live throughout those movies while I
stroll throughout you till I disremember
your entendres and see I'm new-born-baby tender, stepping
through actuality, through you—not a film-
set, O Mountain Brow, where I'll never be panorama-
spoiling, nor granted-takingly peripheralizing
you, while I'm here with others. To others I sing
your graces and discuss your day, that I may sing my
soul-eternal ardour for you—for your verve in a time
of dying—so you may over-hear and feel
esteemed, welcome, invited, O Mountain Brow, where I sing
the Scenic mansions you visit in forms of flower-
blended balmy breezes. I whisperingly-sing to
your peach blooms flashback-fast-bursting in the stilling
air. Pilgrimaging you amid the crimsoning
Staghorn Sumacs swaying, I see: you mean
measurelessly more to me than city-views for
which most others come to you … Vultures,
after cliff-side-congregations—seemingly
free-wheeling feelingly—beat their wings in time

to the waterfall's phantom-eerie hiccupping, to which
anyone may calibrate. O Mountain
Brow, remember those nights, at the Flat Rock, with the San
Boys who hallucinated hundreds of faces
on your Orcus-shadowy crags. How many
first kisses transpire at this look-out—beyond the Ravine-
bounds—whereon I behold the high-wind-blown-stone-for-a-second-
seeming roses, O Mountain Brow, whose Scenic
Drive is never littered as much as other parts
of Hamilton—sometimes Elysium-seemingly
clean? O Mountain Brow, the greying Italian bocce-
ballers playing in the twilight sometimes
soften their footfalls, as though they know that
you can feel, as you do. O Mountain Brow, I even proposed
to a yes-exclaiming girl upon your north-most Ravine-
opposing bench, one time, O Mountain Brow,
where I kneel in prayer upon the purple-bluing pond-
shore sands, O Mountain Brow, where your back-to-life-
welcoming-warm wind once spoke to me through evening
rustles of the oak leaves: "life-long-seeming
kisses will electrify the lilies of
the cliff until they shiver in the fervor
you'll soon feel in this same place." O Mountain Brow,
let us share this daybreak before other
Mountain Browers come … crag-magnetized since boyhood,
I so wish to share this dawn with you, alone.

Judgment Day

for Angela Macaluso

When ray-right-rain-fair Judgment Day does break;
when, upon a purple carpet of cloud-bursts—the moon setting—
the Maker nears His aurora Throne in the wake
of Saint-Cecile-conducted Seraphim trumpeting
His every quintessential motion; When He does
sit on air and deem our every thought and action,
whose names among ours will be sung from the slim Book of Life?
How morning star-core-white-and-burning is your faith in the Son?
When the violet-eye-light-beaming Redeemer does
return, on whom among us will He shine his rife
rays? When you wake soon or sleep unto your
deaths—will you suffice for the Paradise of our Creator?
When Shadows will be cast but no sun will beam,
will you ascend in lonely Lord-light gleaming supreme?

If We Received the Three Almighty-Given

If we'd received the three Almighty-given
wishes we envisaged in Montreal,
après Layton's funeral, in the hotel?
(Or motel? It never mattered where we were,
so long as we were together; whether inside
wide open clearings or Sanatoriums,
we, when one, resided in one place:
our early Heaven—with nothing more to dream.)
After Cohen, ultra-awed in the face
of your visage, we bowed, my whistling,
waltzed—even through the dolorous slums—
toward our room, where we'd speak of wishes.
Now would you wish us back to one at once,
as I'd, or are these verses of a dunce?

2006, 2022

So Boa-Constrictor-Slowly You Move

So boa-constrictor-slowly you move,
exterminators of my humankind!
Some hardly feel their dying and approve
their deaths with stasis, silence; quarantined,
they cheerlead their own Götterdämmerung
while our exterminators now erect
the camps where Fidelitites—the unsung
saints, the Bride of Christ, the final sect,
dressed from head to foot in fealty—
will kneel before the pits; the humanoids
will jeer them from their seeming realty,
sore from their beast-marks—rabid with tirades.
So boa-constrictor-slowly you kill
those who'll deny or receive you with full will.

A Sonnet to the Trinity

for Angela Macaluso

O Violet-Eye-Light-Beaming Trinity,
O how Your Bride of Saints so speed the butterfly-
turning of souls toward You; O how our slavery—
O Star-Far-Eye-Near One—twilights our children to infinity-
incalculably embracing their bondage, to proclaiming
they are free, when, all-the-astral-projection-immeasurable
while, they are slaves who will not free themselves;
slaves who'll wish to rename constellations;
slaves who'll wish for numbering to replace naming;
slaves who'll wish to replace freedom with shaming;
slaves who'll wish for their own cancellations,
therefore, O Redeemer, in your name I am reclaiming
myself for these slaves' reclaimants; in your name I'd die as You've
in mine; help me to die like a lion when time to prove!

Acknowledgements

I would especially like to wholeheartedly thank my extraordinary editor, Anna van Valkenburg, and all the folks at Guernica Editions who have successfully helped me publish this book.

A very special thank you goes to Diane Windsor, since she has inspired this book more than any other person in my life. A massive thank you to this beautiful force of nature, whom I love second only to God—a woman without whose continual encouragement, inspiration, criticism, and love, I would not be the poet I am, today.

About the Author

Marc di Saverio hails from Hamilton, Canada. His poems, translations and artwork have appeared internationally. In Issue 92 of *Canadian Notes and Queries*, di Saverio's *Sanatorium Songs* (2013) was hailed as "the greatest poetry debut from the past 25 years." In 2016, he received the City of Hamilton Arts Award for Best Emerging Writer. In 2017, his work was broadcasted on BBC Radio 3 and he published his first book of translations: *Ship of Gold: The Essential Poems of Émile Nelligan* (Vehicule Press). On May 1st, 2020, Guernica Editions published *Crito Di Volta*, a 200-paged epic poem, to international critical acclaim. Guggenheim Fellow and Griffin Prize Winner AF Moritz wrote: "*Crito di Volta* is a completely original mastery of the art of poetry—a work of genius." Di Saverio studied English and History at McMaster University, but never took a degree, due to illness. He is the son of Carlo Di Saverio, the scholar and teacher who studied Linguistics and Languages at University of Toronto (M.A.,1981). Di Saverio's poem "Weekend Pass" was adapted into the movie *Candy*, directed by Cassandra Cronenberg and starring the author himself, which was selected to the Toronto International Film Festival in 2013. In 2021, he received a Pushcart Prize nomination and he started his first novel, *The Gallops of Glory*. In 2022, he was shortlisted for the Bressani Literary Prize and he was invited to exhibit art at the Carrousel du Louvre in France.